MA.._

CHANGES

NOT

EXCUSES

66 Day Program

On How to Leave Yesterday Behind

Molly Harvey

MAKE

CHANGES

NOT

EXCUSES

---

66 Day Program

On How to Leave Yesterday Behind

Molly Harvey

CONTENTS

DEDICATION

This book is dedicated to

My mother Peggy
Her partner Neil
My young brother James
Wise friends Jim, Gary, Angel Bob,
and Alfie the cat

Your passing over the rainbow bridge in 2018
made me realise it was truly time to
Make Changes NOT Excuses.

ACKNOWLEDGEMENTS

This book came about as a result of my life falling apart in 2014
and I want to extend my deepest gratitude and thanks
to the following people.

My closest friend Louise Griffith whose incredible support
and listening ear helped me get out of bed during days
when I did not want to get up.

Tina Symes, you are truly a Fire Bird, thank you for your friendship, the
food packages and the laughter.

Christine Pedros, you have been there over the last six years by my side
offering emotional support and walking the road of life when there were
days that I could not see the light at the end of the tunnel.

Sylvia Morgan, there are no words to describe your support except to say
'you are the wind beneath my wings in the business'.

My little sister Anna, you have always been a constant in my life, never
judging my decisions and always at the end of a phone with
a listening ear.

Deborah, Anna's daughter, who has such a sharp sense of humour.
Thank you for making me laugh out loud on days where I only saw walls.
You are full of promise.

And finally my partner Paul. My soul recognises your soul. We are the
same, we are ONE. I feel so blessed that we re-found each other and
have fallen deeply in love again this lifetime.

INTRODUCTION

Until 2014, I had never allowed things to stop me or get in my way; family was my number one value. I had been happily married for over twenty-four years, yet something so deep inside of me, call it souls knowing, knew our marriage had come to a NATURAL ending. Life as I had known it came crashing down around me and fell apart over the next 6 years.

I got divorced, moved home four times and in 2018 I was buried alive in an avalanche of grief and sadness when in one year I lost three members of my family, three good friends and Alfie the cat.

Like never before, I had to make changes, not excuses. I had studied human potential over twenty-six years and in this book, I will share with you, over 66 days, how you too can make changes not excuses in your life.

But first, you have to be willing to let go and move through your excuses day by day by starting off each day with this book taking small steps.

This book is my gift to you. Let's walk together through the next 66 days making changes not excuses.

Never forget, you are full of promise.

WEEK ONE

Step Inside

" *Slow down
the universe has
secrets to
tell you.*"

– Molly Harvey

DAY 1

'Slow Down, Surrender to the Universe'

One of the ways I slow down and surrender to the universe is by walking. I love to walk in the fields by our home; it is my contemplative time where I get to be at one with nature. When we allow ourselves to slow down, our imagination comes alive. We all have an incredible imagination. However, in today's world we are very often caught up in 'hurry sickness' allowing no time to stop, pause and ponder.

When we slow down, we stand on the threshold between our inner and outer world… our imagination awakens, and our great friend 'possibility' comes to life. When we get the chance to slow down and surrender, life becomes present to every moment. We begin to live with our feet firmly grounded in reality. Being present is stillness. There is no chaos, just calm.

Seconds to ponder

When you hear the words slow down what happens inside of you?

....

....

....

How do you feel about surrendering to the universe?

....

....

....

ACTION

Put your walking shoes on and get out in NATURE today.

" In stillness lives wisdom. In solitude there is no noise? In silence you will find yourself."

\- Molly Harvey

DAY 2

'Make Time for the Three S's in Life'

(Stillness, Solitude, Silence)

For many years I was a constant 'doer'. Every day I worked from a huge to do list. Sometimes when I did a task that was not on the list, I would add it as it made me feel like I had achieved even more.

Then in 2012 I was asked to be a visionary and sit on the board of the Fountain, which is a movement to restore nature and the sacred by actualising a new economy of sacred economics. I got to travel to many unusual places and sit in circle with many elders from around the world.

Initially I thought I was brought in to be a member of the Fountain to be a connector, and then something extraordinary happened. Over the next six years of being a visionary in the Fountain, I was called to be still, very silent, and at times experience solitude, and through practice I achieved more by doing less.

When we step off the hamster wheel of life and make time for stillness, solitude and silence, our whole inner world opens up and gives us answers to questions we have been asking on the outside for far too long.

Seconds to ponder

How much stillness, solitude and silence time do you put in your diary?

....

....

....

How do you feel when you stop and slow down?

....

....

....

ACTION

Get your diary out and add in stillness, solitude and silence time.

*" Let yourself
be guided by
the still small
voice within."*

\- Molly Harvey

DAY 3

'Let Yourself Be Guided'

To be guided we need to listen. When you listen, you will feel the silence, when you become silent you will hear a whole new level of listening. To let ourselves be guided we need to quieten the ego. The ego likes to keep us busy focussing on problems and struggles. We can get caught up being human doings instead of human beings.

I have found over the years that spending time in silence takes discipline; then I can quieten my mind and cut out the outside noise. Some people find meditation a useful practice in quietening the mind. When I speak about being guided, it means listening and hearing to the inner voice. We have many voices playing in our heads, yet the small, still voice is different. When I hear it, it has a different tone and vibration.

We can also be guided in life by paying attention to what life is showing us in front of our nose. The universe is speaking to us all the time, yet very often we don't listen or pay attention. Many years ago, I was told a beautiful story about a Tibetan doctor. It takes a lot of years to be qualified as a doctor and when they are going to see a patient, they read what is happening in the environment around them as they travel. They can also tell a lot by the pulse of their patient. They are guided by the environment and their senses.

Seconds to ponder

Where in the past do you feel you have been guided?

. . . .

. . . .

. . . .

Did you trust the guidance?

. . . .

. . . .

. . . .

ACTION

Make space in your life to turn inwards and trust your
guidance.

" Sometimes in life our 'Stop Doing' List needs priority over our 'To Do' List."

– Molly Harvey

DAY 4

'Stop Doing Lists'

Have you ever allowed yourself to slow down and look at what drives you so much? Sometimes being always busy can be a form of distraction. Busyness and to do lists can give us a false sense of control but not always the results we really want. I remember when I was a young mother and I thrived on to do lists. I had lists for the business, lists for the home and even a list regarding what needed to be done in the garden.

I first heard of a 'stop doing list' when I attended the National Speakers Association Convention in Dallas. Nido Qubein was the speaker. As he spoke from the stage about useless busyness and always being in a hurry, he then asked the audience how many of them had a 'stop doing list'. Only about two hands went up. I sat there thinking "he is speaking about me, that's my life, I live by to do lists".

The thought of slowing down and having a 'stop doing list' terrified me. Yet deep inside I felt the time had come in my life to slow down and tune into the real truth that would only come to the surface when I gave myself the space and time to sit, reflect, and make a decision about what I needed to stop doing in my life.

Seconds to ponder

How big is your to do list?

....

....

....

Have you got a stop doing list?

....

....

....

What do you want to stop doing that no longer enhances your life?

....

....

....

When will you start your stop doing list?

....

....

....

ACTION

Now grab a pen and paper and write your stop doing list.

" Don't play a victim to the circumstances you created."

– Molly Harvey

DAY 5

'No One is Coming to Rescue You'

Be honest, how often in your life have you played the victim card, the drama queen or thrown the dummy out of the pram? Is this because things may not have gone the way you wanted them to? I have news for you … no one is coming to rescue you.

However, the answer lies within you. Only you can give up the excuses. Only you can make that step change. Only you can choose to let the old story go and from today take action and make the changes you want in your life.

Seconds to ponder

What area of your life are you blaming someone else?

....

....

....

Have you ever been a drama queen, the victim or a moaner?

....

....

....

What small step would you take today that could help you create the life you truly want?

....

....

....

ACTION

Write out your old story, then burn it.

" *Wake up early and learn while the world sleeps.* "

– Molly Harvey

DAY 6

'How You Start Your Day is How You Live Your Day'

One of the reasons I have got up early over the last thirty years is that it gives me the time to ease into the day ahead. No rushing, no phone calls, no emails, just silence.

When we rush into our day, we spend the rest of the day catching up complaining about time. When we allow our self to ease into the day, we find the flow and rhythm of the day ahead. Getting up early also helps you create 'you time', and in that 'you time' you can ponder on the days tasks that need to be achieved.

What I have found over the years is every day brings its own challenges or unexpected problems to be solved. Yet because of the early morning quiet time, I find my mind is more creative and calmer to plan the day ahead. Use the early morning for "you time", a time to be silent, pause, learn and visualise the day ahead.

One of the tiny disciplines I bring into the early morning is to ask myself; "What are the two or three tasks I would like to get done before 5pm this afternoon?" Always do your most difficult task in the morning.

Seconds to ponder

Are you someone who presses the snooze button, or do you jump out of bed to start the day?

....

....

....

Are you willing to set your clock 60 minutes earlier to gain some you time and ease into your day?

....

....

....

ACTION

Set your clock 30 to 60 minutes earlier each morning. Get up, embrace the day. Do it for 66 days. Start from tomorrow morning.

" You must let go to move on to the new story."

– Molly Harvey

DAY 7

'Whatever You Can Let Go of Determines

How High You Can Fly'

In my mentoring practice I have spaces to accept new clients once per quarter. The first assignment that each person receives is a document called 'clean-up to clear out'. This encourages the individual to look at the whole of their lives especially their living space and workspace. I am passionate about letting go of stuff around us so as we can make space for the new.

I encourage you now to walk around your home as if you are seeing it for the very first time.

- Where is the clutter?
- Are the pictures on the wall part of your old story?
- Are your wardrobe and drawers overflowing with clothes and shoes you don't even wear anymore?

To move into the new story, we have to first let yesterday go. Close your eyes visualise each room in your home or apartment, where is the clutter?

Seconds to ponder

Now make a list of each area and what needs to go.

....

....

....

For each item that you are letting go of, ask yourself "is this in my old story or does it belong in the new story?"

....

....

....

See yourself 66 days from today having let go and create space in your new life. Write how it will feel.

....

....

....

ACTION

Grab a black bag. Set the timer for 5 minutes. Walk around your home. What can you let go of right now and in this moment?

" In life, only a few things matter. Know what those few things are."

– Molly Harvey

WEEK TWO

What Do You Really, Really Want?

" *If you really want to do something, you'll find a way. If you don't, you'll find an excuse.* "

– Jim Rohn

DAY 8

'Stop Talking About What You No Longer Want'

When I meet people, they are so good at telling me what they NO longer want in their life and they seem to get great joy out of sharing it over and over again. What they don't realise is when you keep talking about what you don't want in life, it keeps showing up in life. Yes, everything you don't want.

Human beings are just like magnets, we attract what we feel and think about all day long. So, what do you want? Tell me what you really want? Feel into it.

One of the most powerful exercises I do when coaching people is to encourage them to get a piece of paper and draw a line down the middle. On the left-hand side write everything you no longer want in your life, be ruthless. Then on the right-hand side, what do you want.

Seconds to ponder

No longer want	What do I want?

ACTION

Pick one thing from what you want in life and start making it happen today.

" Make changes

not

excuses today."

\- Molly Harvey

DAY 9

'List Your Excuses'

There is something liberating about getting a large blank sheet of paper and write down all the excuses you have let get in the way of living your best life.   Listing the excuses is another way of having fearless conversation with yourself. It helps you realise where in your life you have been playing small until now.

When we run the 'make changes not excuses' workshop, I ask the audience to find a partner and share the number one excuse they let get in the way of living their best life. They then share it and connect deeply and say the words "I am so done with that excuse".

You can feel the vibration and relief change in the room as everyone realises, we all tend to use the same excuses in life.

Seconds to ponder

List your number one excuse that has held you back until now in:

Personal life

. . . .

Business

. . . .

Health

. . . .

Relationship

. . . .

Money

. . . .

ACTION

Make a decision today to let go of your number one excuse that has held you back until now.

" Embrace and own the light that you are.

Step out of the shadows today."

– Molly Harvey

DAY 10

'Step Out of the Shadows'

Step out of the shadows, your light is needed right now in the world.

In August 2016 I flew to Santiago de Compostela Spain with my dearest friend Louise Griffith. Louise and I had walked by each other's sides since we first met at the National Speakers Association in Dallas in 2001. From our first meeting we had a deep soul sister connection; it was as if we had known each other all of our lives and many lives before. So, there we were walking the road in the hot Spanish summer of 2016... little did I know what a profound impact the Camino was to have on my life.

On day five of the walk we were both exhausted and by now my feet were full of blisters. As we walked along the road we stopped at a small café at the side of the road. Louise met a young photographer who came to sit with us. He shared his story of how the Camino had changed his life and he was called to live on the Camino Road and take pictures of the pilgrims in their NATURAL raw state. We were fascinated and he invited us to be part of a group photo with other pilgrims.

At first the voice in my head said, "look at the state of you, no way you're getting your photo taken". Then in the next moment, I got caught up in the adventure of walking out to a barn at the back of the café and joining the group. We all huddled together, and I chose to stand at the back of the group. All of a sudden, the photographer came out from behind the camera and pointed at me... I heard his voice vibrate through my presence "Hey, you at the back! Step out of the shadows. Why are you standing in the shadows?" At that moment I broke down and wept in front of the whole group as I realised that since my marriage broke down two years earlier, I had been living in the shadows.

Seconds to ponder

Are you currently living in the shadows?

....

....

....

Where in your life are you living in the shadows?

....

....

....

What if in this moment, now, today, you stepped up and stepped out. What would it feel like? Do it now!

....

....

....

ACTION

Pick one area of your life where you have been standing in the shadows what action will you take today towards stepping out.

" *Stay curious.*

Banish your

excuses."

– Molly Harvey

DAY 11

'Replace Your Excuses with Curiosity'

Curiosity forces us to explore the truth, face our fears and be honest to ourselves. When you decide to let go of excuses you walk into the unknown.

My grandmother Molly Ormond always encouraged me to be curious and always have the courage to use it. Look at children; they are full of wonder and curiosity. I say spend more time around children, as you end up with them in their playful vibration.

When we are in that state of mind, our minds become like an open parachute and it expands your universe physically and mentally.

Seconds to ponder

Where could you be more curious in life?

....

....

....

Where in the past have you stayed curious and it's had a positive effect?

....

....

....

ACTION

Next time you are making an excuse, pause and lean in with curiosity and take action.

"Losers make excuses. Winners make progress."

– Molly Harvey

DAY 12

'No Excuses Journal'

What if you kept a No Excuse Journal for 66 days? That would mean being truly accountable for your excuses. The excuses that hold you back in life.

Each morning when you wake, open your journal and visualise how good it feels to no longer be letting your excuses get in the way of you living your best life... and as you sit and visualise, you know you are also creating a new story in your life. Be there before you get there. Live every moment in the 66 days as if the excuses are no longer in your life.

If you do let the excuses creep back in again, instead of shaming yourself and feeling bad, just go back to day one and start again. Why do I say go back to day one? Well, when we refuse to let go of old habits or excuses that no longer serve us, it's the consistency of the new habit that makes the difference. I believe it takes about 66 days to give up an excuse. Giving up excuses is all about taking small steps every day in the direction we want our life to go in.

Seconds to ponder

What excuse do you really want to let go of for 66 days?

....

....

....

Imagine you are now at day 66. How do you feel, what changes have happened as a result of not making the excuse?

....

....

....

ACTION

Start a no excuse journal today.

" Stop trying

and

just do it

today."

\- Molly Harvey

DAY 13

'Stop Trying'

Have you ever said the words "I will try to?" It's not good enough; it really means you are never going to do what you said you would do.

I learned that many years ago when I went to a slimming club to lose weight. For the first three weeks everything went well. I was filled with motivation to let go of the excess weight. Then on the fourth week, when the consultant in charge asked me how much weight I wanted to let go of the following week, my answer was "I will try to lose 2lbs". On my way home I went for a curry with a friend. That was the beginning of the end of me attending the slimming club.

Pay attention to your comfort zone as it is your enemy not your friend.

Seconds to ponder

Where in your life have you used the words 'I will try'?

. . . .

. . . .

. . . .

What could you replace the word 'try' with?

. . . .

. . . .

. . . .

ACTION

In one area of your life where will you let go of the word try?

"Ask, Believe, Pay Attention, Receive."

– Molly Harvey

DAY 14

'Ask for a Sign'

Two years ago, I needed to change my car and I asked my partner Paul would he help me find the next car. He was delighted and started to ask all sorts of questions around what the car needed to be. Suddenly looking for a car seemed too much like hard work to me so I told him it must have three things. Number one, it must be an automatic. The second thing that was important to me was that it was black, and the third wish was that the car would have leather seats. All the other details I left to him.

I learned in business many years ago to surround yourself with people who are much better and far cleverer than me in areas where I wasn't. By the end of the day we were driving to view the car of my dreams. On the way I told Paul that I had asked for a sign to let me know this car was the one. As we drove along the M6 in rush hour, there was the first sign, a huge rainbow straight ahead. I said to Paul "I bet where we are going to view the car is at the end of that rainbow". He smiled and just kept driving. When we got to where we were to view the car, it felt like the end of a rainbow. The rainbow had stayed ahead of us during the whole journey.

The second sign was when we sat in the car to test drive it, there was a pair of rosary beads hanging from the mirror, and it reminded me of my Irish roots. The third sign came almost as soon as the engine was switched on. The car had an in-built movie player and Mrs Brown's Boys came on, again another sign related to my background. I have always followed the 'power of three' and I had been given three signs that this was the car I would buy.

We agreed to buy the car and the owner looked at me intensely and said "this car has been incredibly lucky for me as I lost everything a few years ago and when I got back on my feet, I bought the car". He had no idea how much those words meant to me as I too had just been through a tough period of my life. The moral of the story is, ask the universe for a sign then pay attention as she always delivers.

Seconds to ponder

Where in the past have you asked for a sign?

....

....

....

Where currently in your life will you ask for a sign?

....

....

....

ACTION

Pick an area in life or business where you will take action
today and ASK.

" *Be clear on the outcome you want to see in your life.* "

– Molly Harvey

WEEK THREE

Own Your Power

" Every day unlearn and let go of what limited you yesterday."

\- Molly Harvey

DAY 15

'You Are Not Big Boned'

When I was a child, I was overweight and very conscious of it as I entered my teenage years. The term that was used in my family was... "Oh Molly is just big boned, it runs in the family, especially on the women's side".

As I grew into my twenties, I continued to believe I was big boned and that became my excuse for not losing weight. Until in my early forties, I made a conscious choice to give up the excuse and tone up.

I remember one day being on stage and talking to a large audience about limiting beliefs and excuses. I raised my hand up to demonstrate an exercise and I caught a glimpse of my wrist. I realised in that moment my wrist was tiny and that I was not big boned, in fact I had the frame of a small woman. In that moment, years of excuses and a belief that was not even my own, fell away.

Seconds to ponder

What excuses and beliefs are you holding on to that are not even your own?

....

....

....

What will you change from today?

....

....

....

Write down some of the sentences you heard as a child that are not even you.

....

....

....

ACTION

Find an accountability buddy to help you release the past.

*" Get up; take the
next tiny step
when you don't
feel like it."*

\- Molly Harvey

DAY 16

'You Will Never Feel Like It'

Motivation alone very often doesn't work. It works in the short term; however, it is the discipline of the right habits that works in the long term. Let's be honest, when we start any new project it feels great in the beginning but halfway through it very often becomes sticky and challenging. That's when the excuses start like "I don't feel like it". That's when you need to persist and keep going.

Be honest, sometimes you are never going to feel like doing something, but you need to push through and do it anyway. I am encouraging you to lean into your resistance and push through.

I have found in my own life it's the things I haven't very often felt like doing that have been the most rewarding in the end.

Seconds to ponder

Make a list of what you don't feel like doing but know inside that you need to do it.

....

....

....

Now re-list each task. When will you do it?

....

....

....

How do you feel now that you have pushed through your resistance?

....

....

....

ACTION

Reframe your words "I don't feel like it" to "I will do it now".

"Simplify to create space in your life today."

— Molly Harvey

DAY 17

'Less is More'

Mahatma Gandhi said, "Live simply so that others may simply live". Yet for most of us we have too much stuff. The best part of living with less stuff is that the rewards are immediate, you have less to choose from, less to clean, and fewer decisions to make.

There is an old Buddhist story about a man who visits a Zen Master seeking spiritual guidance. Instead of listening, the visitor spoke mainly of his ideas. After a while the master served tea. He filled the visitor's cup and then kept pouring as it spilled on to the table. Surprised, the visitor exclaimed that the cup was full and asked why he kept pouring when nothing more would fit in the cup. The master explained that like the cup, the visitor was already full of his own ideas and opinions and that he wouldn't learn anything until his cup was emptied.

Where in life could you empty your cup?

Seconds to ponder

For you to embrace your space, what could you clear out today?

....

....

....

Less stuff = more freedom. What could you buy less off right now?

....

....

....

The number one reason to keep an article of clothing is to wear it. What have you not worn that's been in your wardrobe for the last 6-12 month? Let it go today.

....

....

....

ACTION

If something new comes into your home, one thing goes out.

" We are all doing our best. Stop beating yourself up when you're trying so hard. It isn't going to help you; just do it better next time."

– Rachel Hollis

DAY 18

'Stop Apologising'

Do you ever find yourself apologising for things you have not even done? Sometimes, as women, we over apologise. Maybe it's time to stop apologising for the things that are not our fault. Over apologising can become a habit that holds you back again and again. You are giving your power away.

Next time you find yourself apologising, pause instead. When a woman starts a statement by saying "sorry but…" it can very often undermine what you were going to say.

Practice never starting a sentence with 'sorry'. Instead, maybe say "I might be wrong, however…"

When someone gives you a complement e.g. "you're looking well" just say thank you.

Seconds to ponder

Think about your language… and catch yourself. In one day, how often do you say "I'm sorry"?

....

....

....

Think back to a situation in the past when you over apologised. How did you feel?

....

....

....

What word could you use instead of the word "sorry" to get your point across?

....

....

....

ACTION

Instead of saying sorry, practice saying "thank you".

" You're not lost. You are just exploring. Get over yourself today."

– Molly Harvey

DAY 19

'Build a Bridge, Get Over Yourself'

For years I have used the sentence "Build a bridge, get over yourself" when facilitating leadership programs. It's a tough sentence yet sometimes in our lives we need to hear it. I call it having a fearless conversation with ourselves.

Without realising it, we can all spiral down at various times in our lives and then we attend pity parties where we bitch, moan and whinge about our circumstances, our health or just life in general. We get caught up in a sea of blame and pettiness.

If you are currently the leader of a pity party, let it go, stop the party. Start a journal and write down a list of what is currently working in your life. Too often we focus on failure and what we don't have in life instead of focussing on what we do have and what's positive.

Start today to build a new bridge in your life.

Seconds to ponder

Why and where do you need to get over yourself right now?

....

....

....

How will you build the new bridge?

....

....

....

Where do you need to stop being a BMW (bitch, moan & whinge)?

....

....

....

ACTION

Have a fearless conversation with your inner self today.

" You can't make everyone happy. You're not an Avocado."

\- Anonymous

DAY 20

'Disease to Please'

Are you a people pleaser? Do you try your hardest to be nice to everyone? So much so that you end up doing jobs that are not even your own? Maybe you put up with energy vampires who spend hours complaining how bad their life is. Maybe you get tangled up with colleagues who just love creating dramas while others seem to avoid that person. You promise yourself you will stay away from them and yet they suck you into their world time and time again.

Being a people pleaser can leave you vulnerable to being manipulated by others who know how to use guilt to get you to accommodate their needs. That in turn gets you stuck in a pattern where you don't want to disappoint them. It distracts you from your purpose, wastes your time and contributes to you being stuck in life.

Sometimes in life, if you are a people pleaser, you will need to work on looking at where in your life you are over functioning. E.g. your desire to be helpful and a reluctance to let others down. Because the effort you put into being helpful and always putting others first, makes you feel like a good person.

The disease to please is anything but pleasant and it can be poisonous for your life and career.

Seconds to ponder

Where in your life currently or in the past have you been a people pleaser?

. . . .

. . . .

. . . .

What will you do from today?

. . . .

. . . .

. . . .

ACTION

Pay attention to what area in your life you have been a people pleaser. Ask yourself why do you do it! Practice taking your power back and say "no" more.

" Be the light that you came here to be."

– Molly Harvey

DAY 21

'Claim Your Achievements'

Why are women much harder on themselves than men? Why, sometimes, do we go out of our way to avoid taking credit for what we have done? Is it because you are afraid that you would be seen as boasting or full of yourself? Reluctance to claim achievements has been something that I have had to work hard at most of my life.

When I was growing up, I remember hearing sentences like "Don't be thinking above your station", "You are an empty vessel that makes a lot of noise". So, when I did leave school, I spent a lot of my life keeping my head down and learning everything I could, never really drawing attention to myself.

As I got older, in the early days of being an international speaker, when someone would say "I am really looking forward to hearing you speak" I heard "You are an amazing speaker". I would usually bypass the comment with the sentence "Well let's see, under promise over deliver", and that would take the limelight off me. Then one day I realised, if I was going to truly move ahead in my speaking career, I had to own my light, show up and take bold action.

Now whenever my achievements are read out before I address a group, I always turn to the person introducing me and I say "Thank You".

Seconds to ponder

Where in your life have you been reluctant to claim your achievements?

. . . .

. . . .

. . . .

What were some of the unhelpful comments said to you?

. . . .

. . . .

. . . .

ACTION

As you walk into the future how can you get better at letting people know your achievements?

"Yesterday ended last night."

— Molly Harvey

WEEK FOUR

Own Your Presence

" *You get to decide who you allow into your inner cathedral. Pay attention to who you open the door to.*"

– Molly Harvey

DAY 22

'When the Past Calls, Let it Go to Voicemail'

Outstanding people talk about and share ideas, average people talk about things, and small minded people gossip about others. Life is too short to get stuck in 'yesterday' and that is where so many of us are. We talk about what happened yesterday, last week, last year, ten years ago and keep replaying the record of what didn't work out.

My motto since being a young adult has been, say sorry quickly, forgive what went wrong and move on, otherwise we let people and things from the past that have hurt us live rent free in our head.

Today I encourage you to take the Bed & Breakfast sign down and when the past calls again, let it go to voicemail.

Seconds to ponder

Who lives rent free in your head?

....

....

....

When will you take the Bed & Breakfast sign down?

....

....

....

Are you outstanding or small minded?

....

....

....

ACTION

When the past calls, let it go to voicemail.

"Make a decision today to be outstanding, not small minded in life."

\- Molly Harvey

DAY 23

'Never Tolerate Toxic Relationships'

For years I have included an exercise in my talks around the five people you hang around with on a 24-hour basis. The exercise gets you to list the five people and then on a scale of 1 to 10, how positive are each of these people in your life. Do they encourage your dreams and aspirations, or do they thrash your ideas and tell you all the reasons why something won't work?

Sometimes in life we can develop unhealthy behaviours and treat each other disrespectfully. Another great question to ask yourself "Is this relationship giving me more than it is taking from me?" If you are in a relationship that sucks the life out of you, remember you are resilient, powerful, kind, and strong. Start to pull away and walk in a new direction.

Never forget that the real you lives beneath your fear. Take the first step today because you become who you have coffee with.

Seconds to ponder

Who are the five people you hang around with on a 24-hour basis?

....

....

....

Now put a number between 1-10. How positive is each person in your life?

Name   1-10 Name   1-10

....

....

....

Are the relationships in your life toxic or healthy?

....

....

....

What actions will you take?

....

....

....

ACTION
Decide today to spend less time in the company of people who drain your life force.

"Daring to set boundaries is about having the courage to love ourselves even when we risk disappointing others."

– Brene Brown

DAY 24

'Create Strong Boundaries'

Very often if you are a people pleaser, you will also be challenged with setting boundaries. In life it's important to set boundaries with others as to what is acceptable and unacceptable in their behaviour towards us. The ability to know our boundaries come from a healthy sense of self-worth.

Setting boundaries is a skill that can be learned. Practice voicing your boundaries, then follow with action. No one has a right to make you feel uncomfortable or take your self-defined space away from you. Very often when something no longer feels right, it starts first in your body. Listen to your body and trust your gut. Speak your truth. Practice pausing or use the power of silence.

Learn to say no to things that just don't feel right. Don't explain, just say no and leave it there. As you practice creating strong boundaries in your life, you will feel a sense of strong self-worth growing inside of you and never forget, you get what you tolerate.

Seconds to ponder

What area of your life do you need to set stronger boundaries?

....

....

....

Why do you need to set boundaries?

....

....

....

How can you be true to yourself?

....

....

....

ACTION

What step can you take today to set new boundaries in your relationships?

"Always trust your inner sat nav. It will take you to where you need to go."

\- Molly Harvey

DAY 25

'Trust Your Inner Sat Nav'

Way back in 2001, I was at a conference in Findhorn and the speaker, Dr Danah Zohir, was speaking about the three brains. As she spoke, every word she said deeply resonated in my gut. She said we had three brains, the head, heart and belly. I know that my belly has a sat nav that has been guiding me all my life.

I can remember as a child, I sometimes knew things before they happened. I never worried about getting lost because I believed I had a compass inside. Trusting your inner sat nav helps you to know yourself deeper. Your intuition is your moral compass that will always protect you. The more you listen to it, the stronger it gets.

Think back for a moment to a time in your life when you just knew something was going to happen, yet you had no logical explanation of it. That is very often your inner sat nav, you know but you cannot logically explain it. To live by your inner sat nav, you need to be self-aware and connected to everything that is happening around you.

Be still, follow your intuition, and go with what your inner sat nav is telling you.

Seconds to ponder

Tune into your inner sat nav. What does your fear say?

. . . .

. . . .

. . . .

What does your spirit say?

. . . .

. . . .

. . . .

What are you here to learn?

. . . .

. . . .

. . . .

ACTION

Think of an area in your life where you are not clear. Close your eyes, ask your inner sat nav the question? Listen for the answer.

" *Every minute you spend wishing you had someone else's life, is a minute you spent wasting yours.*"

– Molly Harvey

DAY 26

'Stop Measuring Yourself Against Others'

Have you ever compared yourself to someone else with thoughts like "why can't I weigh nine stone like she does?" Or "I wish I was as successful as him". Have you ever stopped to realise those thoughts just make you feel jealous, insecure, guilty and sad, all those low vibration feelings and when we allow ourselves to think in that way, we give away our power to the other person.

If you have ever compared yourself to others, I am encouraging you right now to call back your energy, pay attention and focus on your own life. The only person who you will ever really be in competition with is yourself and not what is outside of you. Live every day to be better than yesterday not better than or the same as someone else.

Pay attention to who and what you judge in life because where your energy goes, your attention follows. Once you realise you are comparing yourself to others, stop and pause. Count your blessings instead.

Seconds to ponder

Where in your life have you compared yourself to someone else?

....

....

....

Focus on your strengths. What are your top two strengths?

....

....

....

What actions will you take to stop it in the future?

....

....

....

ACTION

Count your blessings, take you energy, attention and focus back on your own life from today.

"Just as you have a starting time to your day, it's important to have a quitting time."

– Molly Harvey

DAY 27

'Have a Quitting Time Each Day'

Be honest, do you have a quitting time each day when you switch off your phone, laptop, computer and all the outside noise? In a world consumed by hurry sickness, so many people are taking their work home at night or staying much later in the office in the evening. We are human beings not robots. Down time is so important.

Many women I know who are climbing the corporate ladder, go back to work on their laptops at night when the children are in bed, then wonder why in their mid-forties or early fifties, they suffer from burn out. Very often marriages hit the rocks because they have grown apart.

Just as you have a starting time each day, it is so important to have a quitting time. Never take your life for granted, spend time with your partner, family and close friends. Set your quitting time each day and stick with it.

Seconds to ponder

What time each day do you quit work?

....

....

....

How could you be more present to family and friends?

....

....

....

ACTION

Set a quitting time each day on your phone. Stick to it.

" Step out. Be the presence that you came here to be."

– Molly Harvey

DAY 28

'Own Your Presence'

Do you walk into a room and own it? Does the energy of your vibration spill out across the room that you walk into? If not, why not. Presence is not always loud; presence is very often quiet and consistent. Presence is about the value you bring to the table. Owning your presence is all about paying attention, being present in the moment, being true to who you are as a person, and allowing yourself to get out of your own way and shine.

The value of truly accepting who you are is priceless. Presence is a sense of vibration, it's something you sense and know but can never grasp. Our bodies are a living cathedral of presence. The human face is a miniature village of presence. Our face shows whether we have had a hard life or not. When you own your own presence, you allow everyone around you to step forth and own their own light.

Seconds to ponder

Where, right now in your life, are you currently not present?

....

....

....

What does presence mean to you?

....

....

....

What actions will you take to be present in the moment?

....

....

....

ACTION

Practise spending more time being present to everyone you meet today.

" You never know what is enough unless you know what is more than enough."

– William Blake

WEEK FIVE

Own Your Medicine

" If you want more time, freedom and energy, start saying NO."

– Molly Harvey

DAY 29

'You Are More Than Enough'

How would your life change if you believed you were more than enough? When we live from a place of enough each day, we know inside that we are loveable, good enough and kind. For the times you feel you are not good enough or funny enough, remember that 'you are more than enough'.

Have you ever stopped and paused and realised you are unique; you are the only person in this world who will ever have your thumb print. No, you don't look like anyone else and you were never meant to. You are you.

As my great friend Louise Griffith says, "You are one shining light". In fact, that is what she called her company many years ago. She has been the person in my life who has picked me up every time I have fallen down or felt less than enough. We all need a Louise in our lives, and you can be that person for everyone you meet in your life.

Seconds to ponder

Where in the past have you not honoured your own soul?

....

....

....

Write every day until you believe it inside and out 'I am more than enough'.

....

....

....

What old story do you need to let go of to embrace your own new story 'I am more than enough'?

....

....

....

ACTION

Practice from today living as if you honestly believe you are more than enough.

" Tell those close and dear to you that you are going to make changes and when."

– Molly Harvey

DAY 30

'Look NO in the Face'

Are you a people pleaser? Do you sometimes find yourself running all over the place getting everyone else's work done and none of your own? When was the last time you said no to someone? Sometimes in life we need to learn to say no to others so as we can say yes to our own life.

I am sure some of you reading this right now are thinking "That's so selfish". Well I will never forget July 2008, I was at a National Speakers Convention in New York and I was having a really busy year as a speaker. I was exhausted, however I thought I was hiding it so well until a fellow speaker approached me after a break-out session and said "Molly, you need to become a little more selfish. Step back and do some self-care". I remember the word 'selfish' vibrating through my body and it was in that moment I realised that if I didn't add some more self-care time into my diary and change my habits, I would no longer be able to be there for family, friends and clients.

Self-care is not selfish. Think about it for a moment. Would you get into your car and drive it with no fuel? We all need to stop and refuel now and again.

Seconds to ponder

What do you need to say NO to in your life?

. . . .

. . . .

. . . .

What self-care habits could you add to your life?

. . . .

. . . .

. . . .

ACTION

Stop today and make time for a little self-care.

"On the other side of fear lives adventure."

– Molly Harvey

DAY 31

'Walk into Your Fears'

I will never forget the 11th July 2014. Standing at the cash point of a NatWest Bank, I put my debit card in the machine to get the balance on my account. I almost fell to the ground when I saw that I had ten pounds and forty-nine pence left in my personal account. The day before I had left my marriage after 24 years and stepped out of the whole of my life. The invisible friends that got a hold of me that morning were guilt, shame and sadness. They suddenly jumped on my back as I let fear overcome me for four months.

Every day for four months, no matter how sunny it was, all I could see was darkness. Fear lived around every corner until one day in October I woke up and said, "No more". I had to get a hold of this energy that had a hold on my life. As for the three false friends, guilt, shame and sadness, it was time to take down the Bed & Breakfast sign in my head and stop them living rent-free. From that day I started walking into my fears.

When we get the courage to walk into our fears, we find that the fear dissipates; it scurries away and no longer holds you to ransom.

Seconds to ponder

In this moment, complete the exercise below. Explore your fears. Sit down and invite them to have coffee with you.

. . . .

. . . .

. . . .

What are your fears?

. . . .

. . . .

. . . .

What is the one small step you can take today that will help you face your fears?

. . . .

. . . .

. . . .

ACTION

Right now, make a decision to let go of any false friends you might be carrying. You can do it.

" Life is all about how you handle Plan B."

\- Molly Harvey

DAY 32

'How Time'

Have you ever heard of HOW time? I came across the how time concept through Patrick Grove, who is the Chairman of four public companies worth collectively over $1 bn.

In his early days as an entrepreneur, he started a journal about how he was going to reach his goals. Most people ask why and explore the why in their life and business goals, yet not enough of us ask the 'How'.

Patrick began to build how time into his diary, for example, when he was flying from state to state, he would get his journal out and mind map the how's in his business and life.

Seconds to ponder

List your top 3 goals.

· ·

· ·

· ·

Mind map in a blank page journal, 'How' you are going to achieve each goal.

· ·

· ·

· ·

Where will you add in 'How' time to your life?
(Example; mornings, travelling, afternoons etc.)

· ·

· ·

· ·

ACTION

Buy a new journal today and label it your HOW journal.

"Don't be afraid of the answers. Be afraid of not asking the questions."

– Jennifer Hudson

DAY 33

'Ask Great Questions'

Have you ever paused to notice that you never learn anything by talking? You only learn things when you ask questions. Did you ask a lot of questions as a child? My grandmother often said to me when I was young, "How many more questions are you going to ask me before the end of the day?" I can remember being full of curiosity and wonder. Questions wake us up; they prompt new ideas and ways of doing things in our lives.

I learned early on that there are no stupid questions. Asking great questions is positive, productive and creative. It also helps you deeply connect with partners, clients and friends. Good questions are open questions. They cannot be answered by a simple yes or no.

Behind great questions is the ability to listen, answer and suspend judgment. This means being intent on what the other person is really thinking and saying.

Seconds to ponder

When was the last time you asked a great question?

. . . .

. . . .

. . . .

When communicating, do you ask great questions or tell the other person the answer?

. . . .

. . . .

. . . .

Write three great questions you regularly ask other people in your life.

. . . .

. . . .

. . . .

ACTION

Set yourself a target right now. How many great questions are you going to add into your conversations today?

" Cleaning out and decluttering. It could be physical, emotional or spiritual. This will lift your spirits and simplify your life."

– Molly Harvey

DAY 34

'Clear Out Everything in Your Life That Doesn't Lift Your Spirit'

Very often when I take on a new coaching client, the first task I give them is to clear their clutter. That starts with physical clutter in their home and office. I encourage them to make space and to do that, sometimes we need to let go of what no longer lifts our spirits.

I have always passionately believed that when we take control of our home and the space in which we live, we can then begin to re-claim our spirit. It's very often the first step in personal transformation. Clearing the clutter frees up energy and creates space for 'the new' to come into our lives.

Questions to ask yourself as you clear your clutter;
- Do I like it?
- When was the last time I used it?
- If I keep it, where will it be stored?

A great question to ask yourself as you clear out the clutter is, "Does my stuff own me, or do I own my stuff?"

Sometimes our clutter can make us distracted, grumpy and just creates extra work.

Create a plan to spend 10-20 minutes a day clearing. Imagine after 6 weeks the new space you will have created and how much lighter your spirit will be.

Seconds to ponder

Go through your clothes. Ask yourself, "Have I used this item in the last 12 months?" If no, list it on the list below of things to go.

. . . .

. . . .

. . . .

Go into your kitchen, look through cupboards. Take out anything cracked or broken. List below what you will let go of.

. . . .

. . . .

. . . .

How much do you spend on 'stuff' in a week, month, one year?

. . . .

. . . .

. . . .

ACTION

Decide now to clear out some clutter today from one area of your home.

" When you own your medicine, you own your unique gifts and strengths. "

– Molly Harvey

DAY 35

'Own Your Medicine'

Do you own your uniqueness? Do you boldly embrace who you are and what fires you up? Life gets easier when you own your inner confidence. Not the 'fake it until you make it', but the true essence of standing up as to who you are in the world. Has anyone told you lately that you are full of possibility and it's time for you to own your medicine? You are made to celebrate life, owning your personal power and ditch the doubt.

I learned to own my medicine when I was eighteen years old. I went for an interview to attend a course over the winter months all around working with young people in the community. On the interview panel there was a Catholic priest called Father Jimmy O'Connell. He was a wise, reflective quiet man. During the interview he asked me, did I like myself? The question rattled me inside out and my reply was, "I don't know". He then looked at me intensively and said, "Molly, before you hope to work effectively with anyone else, you have to first know and love yourself". That wisdom has stayed with me all my life.

Are you truly ready to own your medicine? Ready to step out in the big world of ours armed with a deep sense of self?

You are ready,

OWN IT!

Seconds to ponder

List the people in your life who support you.

....

....

....

What would you do today if you truly owned your medicine?

....

....

....

List a song that fills you with confidence and helps you own
your medicine (play it today).

....

....

....

ACTION

Google the song that fills you with confidence. Play it, turn
the sound up, dance and move around to it now.

" Your daily behaviour reveals your deepest beliefs."

– Robin Sharma

WEEK SIX

Invite Your Fear to Tea

" Two roads diverged
in a wood and
I took the one
less travelled by,
and that has made
all the difference."

– Robert Frost

DAY 36

'Be the Leader You Want Everyone Else to Be'

Are you the leader of your own life and business? Every year I give many talks and master classes at conferences and organisations, and one of my greatest passions is leadership and encouraging people to be outstanding leaders. To me, that happens by actions and not just talk. In fact, one of my favourite quotes is, "Don't talk about it, just BE" and in our home I have the letters BE on a large picture to remind me every day to BE an example to family, friends and business colleagues.

Do your actions inspire others to learn more, dream more and be more? If so, you are a leader. Leaders demonstrate what's possible. The challenge of a leader is to be humble yet not timid. Be proud but not aggressive. Be kind but not soft. Leadership is a behaviour we live every day.

Seconds to ponder

Are you more effective in a group or on a one-to-one basis?

....

....

....

What makes you special?

....

....

....

How do you want to be remembered?

....

....

....

ACTION

Today practice speaking less and 'being' more; let the essence of your presence shine in everything you say and do.

" Don't compromise yourself, be who you came here to be."

\- Molly Harvey

DAY 37

'It Takes Courage to Move Away From the

Mainstream and Choose a Different Life'

My son Declan inspires me every day because he has always had the courage to walk the road less travelled in life. He made a decision to follow his internal call at a young age. He grew his hair and a long ginger beard and made a choice to step out of school and take a year of thinking time. Most family and friends were shocked and encouraged him to come back and walk with the mainstream. I often heard family say to him words like "cut your hair", "shave your beard", "get a life", "get a job", and he would just look at them in a compassionate way and smile.

As a mother I knew I needed to hold space in a non-judgemental way, for a young man who has had great courage not to give in to the noise outside of himself, and rise above the negativity around him by being uninterested in other's comments.

Never dim your light to please others. Inside each of us we have a destiny to fulfil. It takes courage to move away from the mainstream and choose a different life.

Seconds to ponder

Where in your life have you let what others think of you get in the way?

. . . .

. . . .

. . . .

Right now, where in your life are you dimming the light that you are?

. . . .

. . . .

. . . .

What actions will you take today?

. . . .

. . . .

. . . .

ACTION

Practice being more of your true self today.

" It's not the mountain we conquer, but ourselves."

— Sir Edmund Hilary

DAY 38

'The Only Mountain You Will Ever Have

to Conquer is You'

How do you feel when you have had to conquer your own mountain in life? Are you someone who walks through the fear and keeps on walking, or are you someone who turns your back to the mountain and pretends it's not really there? If you are the person that turns their back to the mountain, remember you and only you have the power to change that. When we find the courage to turn inwards and face the mountain in front of us, we very often find that the fears, doubts and terror start to shrink, and become smaller as you take one moment, one breath and one step at a time. Just put one foot in front of the other and walk.

The journey inward of conquering your mountain will take you to new and exciting places as well as to the depth of your heart.

Seconds to ponder

What inner mountain do you need to conquer?

....

....

....

Are you facing the mountain or are you turning your back on it?

....

....

....

How might you feel once you have conquered it?

....

....

....

What is the worst step you need to take?

....

....

....

ACTION

Today look at the whole of your life, pick an area where you have not been taking action and take the next step.

" *You teach people how to treat you by what you allow, what you stop, what you reinforce.*"

– Tony Gaskins

DAY 39

'You Get What You TOLERATE'

Too often in life we tolerate too much from the past. We settle for the way we have been treated by others. We tolerate procrastination and apathy and very often we walk around numb, not feeling fully connected to source.

Pause as you read today's words and look back for a moment at the past few years of your life, where have you just tolerated bad behaviour of others or accepted less from your life? Make a conscious effort to change small things each and every day and take your personal power back into your hands.

Never forget, you get what you expect, and you deserve what you tolerate.

Seconds to ponder

Where in your life have you been tolerating less than you deserve?

....

....

....

What small steps will you take to stop it?

....

....

....

When will you start?

....

....

....

ACTION

Today act in an area of your life where you have been procrastinating.

*" You cannot
live in today
unless you let go
of yesterday."*

\- Molly Harvey

DAY 40

'Let Go of Yesterday'

Yesterday ended last night yet for most human beings they carry the baggage of yesterday around with them into the present moment and into the future. Pay attention to the conversations you have over the next few days. Observe yourself and notice that when you speak about the past, you find that you are still carrying the past around.

Too often our memories and experiences from the past stifle our present and even our future. I often say to clients, "The past is over, it cannot hurt you". Look for the blessings in the bad experiences then make a decision to move on with your life. You cannot change the past. However, you can make new choices in the present and in the future that you have yet to live.

Seconds to ponder

What memories and experiences do you need to stop carrying around?

....

....

....

Imagine and write how good it will feel to leave it behind.

....

....

....

Find the blessings in the experience or the memory.

....

....

....

Write a note to the memory, or experience thanking it and letting it go.

....

....

....

ACTION

Pay attention to your conversations today, how many times are you talking about the past.

" Stop letting your limiting beliefs live rent free in your head."

– Molly Harvey

DAY 41

'Your Limits are the Lies You Have Told Yourself'

Who limits your life? Look in the mirror right now and ask yourself the question "Who limits me?" Let the mirror speak back, I bet it will say, "You limit yourself". Limits are just thoughts and beliefs that you can, at any time choose to change and let go of. However, you have to be willing to let go of your old story first.

Sometimes we don't consciously realise it, but the story we tell ourselves over and over again is limiting us. Maybe it's time to tell the voice in your head to take a holiday. Always remember, the voice in your head does not belong to you.

Seconds to ponder

Where, right now in your life, are you limiting yourself?

· ·

· ·

· ·

What will it take to let go of the old story you keep telling yourself?

· ·

· ·

· ·

Think of a time you expected something to happen and you set limits around it and it didn't happen.

· ·

· ·

· ·

Think of a time you expected something to happen and you had no doubts or limits and it happened.

· ·

· ·

· ·

ACTION

Make a decision today to let go of one limiting belief.

" The magic lies in your daily routines. "

– Molly Harvey

DAY 42

'30 x 30 x 30 Rule'

Since I was young I have always believed that how you start your day is how you live your day. I learned that piece of wisdom from my grandmother who was an early riser. She was always out of bed with the sunrise and had most of her housework done by 6am. The fire was lit, the kitchen floor was swept, and washed and all the beds in the house were made. She always believed that the early morning was sacred time where in the silence of the new day you could achieve your best work. Her influence was so strong that it lives in me today.

Most mornings I am awake at 5am and my day begins. As my feet touch the floor in the early morning, my first words are "Thank you". Then I head downstairs to the kitchen to feed the cats Grace and Mylo, put the kettle on and make a brew. Then my 30 x 30 x 30 rule begins. 30 minutes of deep silence.

Sometimes I light a candle as I absorb the silence of the early morning and after that I fall into the second 30 minutes of deep learning. I often joke with audiences that I learn when the world sleeps. Some mornings I will read a chapter of a book or start to visualise the day ahead. The last 30 minutes is all about movement. I especially love the bright early mornings from April onwards as I get out and walk.

Sometimes, some of the best ideas can happen when you get out there amongst nature. Let the land around you speak to you, clear your mind and embrace the early morning. It has stories to tell you.

Seconds to ponder

How might your life change if you added 30 minutes of silence each day?

....

....

....

How might your life improve if you added in learning time of 30 minutes each day?

....

....

....

How might your mind and body change if you added more movement to your day?

....

....

....

ACTION

Practice 30 minutes of silence.

" Discipline is the bridge between goals and accomplishment."

\- Jim Rohn

WEEK SEVEN

Create a
New Story

"Let go of who you think you're supposed to be and embrace who you are."

– Brene Brown

DAY 43

'Why Do You Let Your Excuses Get in the Way?'

Your ability and willingness to discipline yourself to accept responsibility for your life is essential. For both your private life and your work life.

A few years ago, I had a great revelation. Every year in my New Year goals, I added 'exercise more' to the dream board and I would feel really motivated for about a month, then the excuses would come back in and I would no longer be going to the gym, so nothing changed. The months turned into years and one day I realised that unless I changed, nothing was going to change. I was responsible and I could no longer blame my lack of exercise on my childhood or the excuses I had made in the past.

The very next day I started walking and after about thirty days, I realised I really enjoyed it. After walking for one year I added Pilate classes to my exercise routine. I realised very quickly that the women who came regularly to class were fit, toned and full of vitality and felt good about their bodies. The women who came ad hoc were overweight and unfit. In that moment I made a decision to give up the excuses and model myself on the women that were fit and toned. To do that it meant I had to show up for class two evenings a week. Every week I grew lighter at the thought of being fit, toned and full of vitality.

Seconds to ponder

Until now, why have you let excuses get in the way?

....

....

....

Where do you need to be more responsible?

....

....

....

Where in your life should you be more self-disciplined?

....

....

....

What's the next action you will take today?

....

....

....

ACTION

If you are not fit, model yourself on someone who is fit, toned and full of vitality.

" The only thing standing between you and your excuses are the lies you keep telling yourself."

– Molly Harvey

DAY 44

'What Will Your New Story Look Like?'

Who is the new you? To create something new we must be willing to let go of yesterday. Start dreaming bigger than you have ever allowed yourself to dream before. From this moment let go and embrace the new story that is emerging from within you.

The new story is all about being worthy and living from that place every day. Dig deep and allow your new story to blossom. Spend time alone and let your intuition speak to you. Stillness is not about focussing on nothingness, it is about creating space for your new story to emerge.

Seconds to ponder

What will your new story look like?

....

....

....

How does it feel to think about the new story?

....

....

....

ACTION

From today, live, feel and breathe the new story as if it's already here.

" Focus only on what's important. Do it now."

– Molly Harvey

DAY 45

'It's Never too Late to Start Today'

Tomorrow is just as busy as today that's why you need to take action today. Where in your life have you made promises to yourself and others that as soon as you stop being busy, you will start? Yet time and life passes by and before you know it you are already another year older and just as busy. Nothing changes until we change and that means letting go of yesterday and the patterns that used to work.

Sometimes we get caught up in the 'good enough' trap and then we tend to take life and work easy and make excuses about starting another day. Get over your excuses and start now, start today.

Seconds to ponder

Where in life or business have you been putting off starting something you should be doing?

. . . .

. . . .

. . . .

List how good it will feel that you have started.

. . . .

. . . .

. . . .

What is the one thing you will start today?

. . . .

. . . .

. . . .

ACTION

Don't talk about it, just start today.

" When you have the courage to live a whole-hearted life, you can write your own story."

— Molly Harvey

DAY 46

'Living a Whole-Hearted Life'

Are you living a whole-hearted life? To live a whole-hearted life is to trust the essence of your own presence. Being present in the moment and owning your own story sounds so easy. Yet it is very hard to do it consistently. It takes courage, grace and compassion to own our worthiness and not get side-tracked by the opinions and judgements of people around us.

One of the main things we have to consistently do if we are going to live a whole-hearted life is to let go of what other people think of you. That means that you might not always fit in with society and everyone around you but it's all about letting go of what people think and embracing who you truly are.

Seconds to ponder

On a scale of 1 to 10, how much do you like and love yourself? (1=low, 10=high)

1   2   3   4   5   6   7   8   9   10

What small changes could you make today to step deeper into living a whole-hearted life?

. . . .

. . . .

. . . .

ACTION

Practice letting go of numbing, cultivate hope, and critical awareness from today. Critical awareness is all about putting things into perspective and realising that you are worthwhile. You are more than enough.

" It is never too late to rewrite your future. Do it today."

\- Molly Harvey

DAY 47

'What Do You Want to Be For the Rest of Your Life?'

Think back for a moment to your childhood years. What did you dream of becoming? What games did you play? I can remember being about eleven years old and one evening, while I was on my way home from school, I stopped by a huge oak tree and sat under it in the middle of a field. I was a day dreamer so as I sat under the tree, I began to imagine that the fields in front of me were filled with hundreds of people. I could see their faces smiling and then the still small voice said to me, "speak, just speak", and I remember speaking to the hundreds of imaginary faces in front of me.

Little did I know, I was already being prepared for the work I do today as a global speaker. Every day we awake to a new day, a day in which we get to make conscious choices. If you are not currently happy with what you are doing in your life, start dreaming, start asking the question, "what is it I really, really want to do?"

Seconds to ponder

Think back to your childhood years. What did you want to be or do when you grew up?

....
....
....

What is it you want to do for the rest of your life?

....
....
....

ACTION

Write one goal you will work towards for the rest of this year.

" Mundane work is hard. Excuses are easy."

\- Molly Harvey

DAY 48

'Every Positive Action that is Easy to Do is Also Easy Not to Do'

It's the positive easy actions/decisions that you make every day that will make a major difference over time. That's the macro picture. However at the micro level we are aware that missing the positive action just once, e.g. having the next cigarette won't make a significant difference to your health.

The danger is we focus on the micro level. We say to ourselves "Oh, one more won't make any difference". We need to focus on the big picture. The positive actions over time will create incredible results.

My partner Paul has been going to the gym four mornings a week for over thirty years. To miss one weeks training won't make a difference to his overall fitness, but that's not the point. Maintain those good habits and the payback can be life changing.

Seconds to ponder

What small daily action could you take that would make a remarkable difference over time?

· ·

· ·

· ·

What could you do today that is very simple but could make all the difference 12 months from today?

· ·

· ·

· ·

ACTION

Everything that is easy to do is also easy not to do. Take action on the mundane today.

" Your world is the outcome of what you pay attention to."

– Molly Harvey

DAY 49

'Zen Like Focus'

Where our awareness goes our energy goes. Yet for most people today they get caught up in distractions and become overwhelmed, never having enough time.

Slow down, pause, get your diary out and ask yourself, "Why am I doing all these things in my diary, are they necessary?" If it isn't necessary, clear it out from your diary and change how you work. Move to working one task at a time. Concentrate, keep your awareness on the task you are focussing on, cut out distraction and develop a zen like focus over a small number of important things.

Life is about balance. Direct your energy to the people and things in your life that truly matter.

Seconds to ponder

What is the one thing you need to focus on now?

....

....

....

How will you feel once you have achieved it?

....

....

....

ACTION

Get your diary out and ask yourself this question, "Is what's in my diary taking me closer or away from where I need to be?" If it is taking you away, dump it from your diary.

*" Step inside
and dance with the
greatness inside
of you today."*

– Molly Harvey

WEEK EIGHT

Small Steps
Every Day

*" Small steps
every day
over time creates
remarkable results."*

– Molly Harvey

DAY 50

'Show Up in Your Greatness'

In 2014, overnight my whole life came crashing down around me. I had been happily married for twenty-four years and I suddenly realised our marriage was over. We had come to the end of the road. I moved out of our home on the 11th July and my face had broken out in a rash over the shame and sadness I felt inside of me. I certainly did not feel great, I felt alone and terrified that it would have been easier to stay and yet I knew deep inside I had to go. I had to find myself again amongst all the chaos and brokenness around me.

Over the next few months and years, I began to re find my greatness again. Little did I know, but when I was most vulnerable in life was where my greatness was hidden. I began very slowly, through my heartbreak, to show up again in the world in my greatness.

Sometimes in life, to show up in our greatness, we need to take off our armour and let go of yesterday, and live the one life we have with courage, purpose and grace.

Seconds to ponder

On a scale of 1 to 10, are you currently showing up in your greatness? (1=low, 10=high)

1   2   3   4   5   6   7   8   9   10

If you are not showing up right now in your greatness, what's stopping you?

. . . .

. . . .

. . . .

ACTION

For the next 66 days, use the following affirmation every day. "I have greatness inside of me".

" *You have greatness within you, let it shine in your presence today.*"

– Molly Harvey

DAY 51

'Take the Next Step Today'

Very often when we decide to give up an excuse, we want to get it out of our life right there and then. For example, you decide to lose weight, so you go to a slimming club or start a nine-day detox where you starve yourself. You dump everything out of your fridge, and you want to be fourteen lbs lighter all in the same day. Time and time again we lose the weight only to put it all back on and more besides. I used to live life that way until I realised that small steps over time was the only way weight was going to stay off for good.

Remember, you don't have to always make massive amounts of progress in one day. The important thing is that you are consistently moving in the right direction. Never under-estimate the power of small daily steps, you will find yourself accomplishing things you never thought possible and sooner than you think.

Seconds to ponder

Where in your life, right now, could you add the small steps principle?

....

....

....

How will you feel when you have achieved the goal?

....

....

....

What is the next right step?

....

....

....

ACTION

Add more consistency to your life from today. Small steps every day matter.

" Empty vessels make the greatest sound."

– William Shakespeare

DAY 52

'Empty Vessels are Genius'

Has anyone ever tried to shame you and make you feel worthless? For years I carried in my invisible backpack, the memory of what happened to me at high school. I always talked a lot in Mrs Kelly's home economics class; I used to get bored quickly so I would start talking to whoever sat next to me in class. As a result, Mrs Kelly would ask me to leave the class and stand outside the door as punishment. One day I found myself standing outside the classroom again, and along walked the principle, Mr Timmins. He just had that way of looking at you that made you feel worthless. As Mr Timmins passed me in the corridor, he muttered the words under his breath, "Empty vessels make a lot of noise".

I can still remember that moment today where I felt shame creep through my body. That shame kept me small for many years until one day I was ready to reframe the bad memory. I reframed the words he had spoken to me, "Empty vessels are genius". In that moment I was free of the past and realised that even at school I was preparing for the future I had yet to live as a professional speaker.

Watch your words, as you never know the impact they could have on someone else.

Seconds to ponder

List some of the shame-based thoughts you might have carried until today?

. . . .

. . . .

. . . .

Reframe to the positive each of the thoughts above.

. . . .

. . . .

. . . .

Who would you be if you let go of those thoughts today?

. . . .

. . . .

. . . .

ACTION

What memories could you reframe in your life?

" If you want to make changes in your life, start by changing your daily habits."

– Molly Harvey

DAY 53

'Create New Daily Habits'

Positive daily habits prime you for success. They help you achieve more, get rid of brain fog and think clearly. For over twenty-five years I have been fascinated by habits and how they affect success. Habits are all about routines that you do repeatedly. When you want to add a new habit in your life, it takes discipline and that means getting the task done whether you feel like it or not.

To get this book completed I had to add a new habit into my life and that was as soon as I got up in the morning, which usually is around 5.05am, get downstairs, make a coffee and write for sixty minutes.

For me, focus is usually great first thing in the morning. Get to know your up time and down time. As my up time is in the early morning, that is when my concentration and creativity is at its best, so that is why I write at that time. When we create new daily habits, we let go of endless distraction, procrastination and start to appreciate the gift of time.

Seconds to ponder

What have you committed to doing that you are currently not doing?

. . . .

. . . .

. . . .

What is the one new habit you would like to add to your life?

. . . .

. . . .

. . . .

What is the one habit you will stop doing in your life?

. . . .

. . . .

. . . .

ACTION

Close your eyes and visualise one new habit in your life, see it, feel it and be it in your life now.

" You can't take it with you. There are no pockets in a shroud."

– Elsie De Wolfe

DAY 54

'A Hearse Never Has a Trailer Behind It'

Sometimes we hold on to clutter out of procrastination and fear, yet we come into this world naked and when the time comes to leave, we can never take anything with us.

When my mother passed away, one of her dying wishes was as the coffin would leave the church we were to play the song 'We Go Out the Same Way We Came In' by Big Tom. At first the family said "no way", however they realised that it was how my mother wanted to be remembered as the words of the song say,

"We're going out the same way we came in
Don't matter who you know or where you've been
Makes no difference who you are
Skid row Joe or super star
You're going out the same way you came in."

We are born into this world without a thing and we leave it naked as we came.

One harsh way to look at your clutter is to imagine the time and energy you will save a loved one by cleaning out your junk before you die. Consider how much peace, simplicity and space you will have in your life while you are still alive.

Seconds to ponder

List 9 things you can put in a black bag and let go of today.

....

....

....

Make a list of each room in your home. What will you let go of over the next six weeks?

....

....

....

Pick one thing you really like and choose who you will gift it to today.

....

....

....

ACTION

Clear some more clutter today.

" Give yourself permission to live a big life."

– Molly Harvey

DAY 55

'Play Big'

Where, right now are you playing small in your life? We all play small somewhere in our lives. Maybe you have stopped playing small in relationships or you are playing small with your health and fitness. The only way to stop playing small is to step back and look at all the areas of your life and challenge yourself.

A lot of times, when we rise up in one area of our lives, we shrink in another. Never play small; it's just as easy to play big as it is to play small. It takes the same amount of energy. Play big in life and stand up and be seen. There is nothing to fear. When we play big, we honour our inner voice and live the call of our soul.

Seconds to ponder

Where, right now in life are you playing small?

....

....

....

Where, right now, are you playing big?

....

....

....

What will you change from today?

....

....

....

ACTION

Make a decision right now to live big and play big in life.

" When someone or something makes you feel small, own your space."

– Molly Harvey

DAY 56

'Stop Addictions That Keep You Small'

Have you ever been in the company of another person, and when you get up from the conversation you feel small? It might be that the person lets you know you haven't worked hard enough; you are not making the amount of money they make. You just don't feel good enough anymore. Throughout life we have all sat in both chairs. There will have been times in the past when you will have made others feel small.

Always remember, no one can make you feel small unless you allow that to happen. Sometimes our ego gets in the way. Learn to shake it off and move on. Ask more questions and listen to the person who is making you feel so small. Maybe it's all in your head. By being disarming and humble, you will actually walk away bigger. Let your life speak for itself.

Seconds to ponder

Think of a time you felt small.

....

....

....

How did you take your power back?

....

....

....

What action will you take in future situations?

....

....

....

ACTION

Own your space today.

" The visionary starts with a clean sheet of paper, and re-imagines the world."

— Molly Harvey

WEEK NINE

Pause and Be Grateful

" Spend the whole day without complaining. Then watch how your life starts to change."

– Molly Harvey

DAY 57

'Visioneering'

When we hold a vision of the future we have yet to live, it helps us look beyond the ordinary. We can dream of the possibilities that are yet to become part of our lives. When you write your intentions down for the future, you then take small steps every day in that direction. It gives your life more meaning. However, as a visioneer, you know it is on its way.

Everything you do, you see first in your mind. Another way of visioneering is to create a vision board. Display your future vision by picking out photos and pictures that represent the life you want to create. It can be a powerful motivator to help you achieve your goal.

Seconds to ponder

Is your vision of the future big enough?

....

....

....

Where do you want to be five years from today? Visioneer it.

....

....

....

What action will you take on creating your future today?

....

....

....

ACTION

Get a blank sheet of paper and draw your future today.

"The visioneer starts with a blank sheet and allows the vision to come alive on the paper."

– Molly Harvey

DAY 58

'Never Complain, Light a Candle'

I have always been allergic to complaining. To me, complaining is a complete waste of energy and when we complain, it just ends up attracting more negativity into our lives. Complaining solves nothing, and it very often sets us on a downward spiral.

Have you ever noticed that when you complain, you very often draw a lot of other complainers into your life without realising it? Complaining becomes a habit. Next time you notice yourself joining in a negative conversation, ask yourself, "Is this conversation enriching my life?" If not, focus your time on something positive.

Every day you spend time complaining is time wasted that you will never get back. If you find yourself complaining about experiences, people and events that happened yesterday, last year, or ten years ago, then it's time to shut up and move on. Why not start this new day by making a decision to stop complaining and light a candle instead.

Seconds to ponder

When was the last time you complained?

. . . .

. . . .

. . . .

Make a list of the complaints.

. . . .

. . . .

. . . .

How did you feel? Had you complained about the same thing before?

. . . .

. . . .

. . . .

What are you going to do from this day onwards?

. . . .

. . . .

. . . .

ACTION

Watch your words and conversations for the next 24 hours; see how many times you complain.

"Journal writing is a doorway to your inner cathedral."

– Molly Harvey

DAY 59

'Journal Every Day'

As I look back on my life, I realise I started to keep a journal from seven years old. Even back then, my journal was my forever friend. I wrote in it when I was happy, sad or challenged. My deepest inner dreams and secrets where all shared in my journal. I remember my journal had a lock and key and I kept the key hidden in a secret place.

Over the years my journal has progressed to the lessons I learned during my divorce and more recently, the deaths of close members of my family. Journaling is a habit, yet don't get stressed if at first you don't journal every day. Writing helps me to process and heal from the trials and tribulations that life throws at us. Most of all, journaling helps you reflect on where you used to be and where you are at this moment in your life.

If you don't already journal then buy yourself a really nice notebook, one you love to look at. Set aside five to ten minutes in the early morning to let your thoughts, feelings and emotions fall onto the blank sheets of paper. Cultivate an attitude of gratitude by listing three to six things you are currently grateful for in your life. Keep your gratitude in a separate section of the notebook and on those days you don't feel so positive, you can look back and watch how your mood and energy will turn to joy and gratitude.

We all have good days and anxious days. When you use a journal during the highs and lows of life, you will step inside to your own inner cathedral of peace.

Seconds to ponder

When was the last time you journaled?

....

....

....

How did it make you feel?

....

....

....

List 3 ways in which journaling enriched or would add to your life.

1. ....

2. ....

3. ....

ACTION

Treat yourself to a new life journal today.

"The death of ego is your possibility of life. Ego is just a dead crust around you. It has to be broken and thrown away."

– Molly Harvey

DAY 60

'Kill Your Ego Every Day'

The ego is a thick veil between what you think you are and what you actually are. Very often we live under the illusion of the mind, and the mind can play tricks on us. Our lives are very often an expression of our inner emptiness.

The artist Marina Abramovic once said, that the moment we believe in our own greatness is when we kill our ability to be truly grateful. Sometime the way of self-absorption ruins the very thing it celebrates.

So, how do you kill your ego every day?

1. Know what matters to you and ruthlessly say no to everything else.
2. Always have the mindset of a learner. No one likes 'know it alls'.
3. Make time every day to meditate.
4. Stop talking, do the work.

Many of us waste too much time talking, endlessly on social media, getting validation and attention with fake likes and attention. Just get on with the work.

Seconds to ponder

Who do you think you are?

. . . .

. . . .

. . . .

Who are you really?

. . . .

. . . .

. . . .

What does your presence say about you?

. . . .

. . . .

. . . .

ACTION

Watch your words and actions today. How many times are you coming from ego rather than the heart?

"Live each season as it passes. Breathe the air, drink the Drink. Taste the fruit and resign yourself to the influence of the earth."

– Henry David Thoreau

DAY 61

'Pay Attention to Nature'

As a child, I grew up on a country estate in Co. Waterford, Ireland. I always felt at one with nature. My childhood was filled with simplicity. I spent many long summers catching tadpoles in small ponds and streams putting them in jam jars, and down by the river catching stickle backs. It wasn't until many years later I realised how lucky I was and spent the rest of my life, until I was fifty-three years old, trying to get back to that simplicity and nature. Then last year, my partner and I moved to a home where the back of the house was all glass and nature and the house are one. I began to live by the seasons again and pay attention to the wonder and mystery of nature.

Simple ways you can pay attention to nature:

- Get out and walk.
  If you live in a city, find a park, sit on a bench and just soak up the beauty around you. If you live in a village, make it a habit of walking in the woods close to you. As you walk, stop and hug a big tree.

- Be present in the moment.
  Read the signs of what nature is saying around you. Notice the weather as you walk, is the wind blowing or the sun shining. If it's raining, pay attention to the raindrops as they fall on your face. Practice meditation with nature, just feel and let yourself dissolve into nature and your stresses and strains will fall away.

Seconds to ponder

When was the last time you went walking in nature?

....

....

....

How present were you to the moment, just enjoying one moment after another?

....

....

....

What do you see, hear, feel, and think?

....

....

....

Set a date now when you will walk in nature.

....

....

....

ACTION

Make some time today to go for a walk.

"Every morning that your feet touch the floor is another opportunity to write a new story."

– Molly Harvey

DAY 62

'Live the New Story'

Every morning that you awake and as your feet touch the floor, is a new opportunity for you to start again. To truly live a new story, we have to first be willing to leave yesterday in yesterday. Yesterday is over, learn from it and not dwell on it. It takes courage and grit to sometimes say "Enough, I am ready to step into the new story". To do that you might need to disconnect for a while from people around you, forgive yourself and forgive those who have wronged you.

If you have been hurt by someone, the last thing you might want to do is forgive, yet it is essential for your spiritual growth and peace of mind. Once you let go, you will find no place for anger and resentment. Then, and only then, will you be able to move on.

I find that when I focus on the present instead of reliving yesterday, you can and will enjoy the present moment more. Learn a new skill, do something different, go somewhere you have never been before, get on and make new friends, make new memories that will become part of your new story.

Seconds to ponder

What is holding you back from living a new story?

....

....

....

What do you need to give up and let go of?

....

....

....

What will your new story look like?

....

....

....

ACTION

Take the next step today in stepping into your new story.

" Open your eyes, look around. Opportunity is everywhere."

– Molly Harvey

DAY 63

'See Opportunity Everywhere'

Very often, my opening words when I speak on leadership are, "The leaders of today and tomorrow are those that can find opportunity in chaos. Opportunity is everywhere". There is no way we can avoid problems in our lives, however depending on how we learn to reframe things, we can find opportunity in every problem we meet in life.

To see more opportunities in life, we have to sometimes slow down, pause and avoid knee jerk decisions. It's important to embrace whatever life throws at us and remember there is always an opportunity in it. In uncertain times, stay flexible and adapt quickly. Take action once you see the opportunity.

Seconds to ponder

Where, right now in your life is there opportunity?

....

....

....

Think of a recent challenging situation you had. Where was the opportunity in that?

....

....

....

What can you do to be more open to seeing opportunities everywhere?

....

....

....

ACTION

Notice and pay attention today to where the opportunities are unfolding around you.

"May your day be filled with wonder. May you have the courage today to stop putting your dreams on hold and make your 'someday' wishes come true today."

– Molly Harvey

WEEK TEN

Don't talk about it, Be it.

" Yesterday is over. Today is full of promise."

– Molly Harvey

DAY 64

'Make Your Some-Day, Today'

Every morning is an invitation and a new blessing. Yet most people live their life not in the present, but always hankering after some-day way in the distant future. You don't have some-day, it's not here yet. However, you do have today and it's a blessing.

What if you awoke every morning and saw each new day as an invitation. No day is ever the same and no day stands still. Each day is unique and different. Why not make your some-day today and live in the presence of this day full of adventure, and let the day unfold.

Spontaneous as in John O'Donoghue's poem 'Fluent'; "I would love to live like a river flows, carried by the surprise of its own unfolding".

Seconds to ponder

What are the dreams and aspirations you are putting off until 'some-day'?

....

....

....

What one thing will you do this day to move towards those dreams?

....

....

....

How will you feel when you have taken action?

....

....

....

ACTION

Bring the future into the present and make your someday today.

" I will prepare and someday my chance will come."

– Abraham Lincoln

DAY 65

'You Are Full of Promise'

Those five words I first heard from Bob Danzig at a National Speakers Convention in Dallas, USA, in 2001. I was new to the speaking game and I met Bob one morning at breakfast. As we ate breakfast, I was fascinated by this man's wisdom and knowledge. I hung on to every word he spoke. At one point in the conversation, he went on to say the words, "You are full of promise". The tears ran down my face as no one had ever said those words to me before.

Then he went on to tell me stories about his life and how a lady called Margaret Mahoney had hired him when he was seventeen years old as an office boy. When she was interviewing him, she ticked him off for keeping his hat on. He then told her he has never worn a hat before, it was his first time and that he didn't know that he was to take it off when being interviewed. She hired him anyway and told him he was full of promise.

Bob rose through the ranks of Hearst Newspaper and eventually became the CEO for over two decades. Bob never forgot those words, "I believe you are full of promise" and continues to pass on those words on to others throughout his lifetime.

Seconds to ponder

Do you believe "You are full of promise"?

....

....

....

On a scale of 1 to 10, how much do you believe you are full of promise? (1=low, 10=high)

1   2   3   4   5   6   7   8   9   10

What needs to happen for you to live the rest of your life believing "You are full of promise"?

....

....

....

ACTION

Say the words to yourself 9 times today, "I am full of promise".

" In a gentle way you can shake the world."

– Mahatma Gandhi

DAY 66

'The World Needs Your Voice Right Now'

The world needs to hear your voice. Yes I said it, your voice, deep inside of you lies a calling unique to you. There is no safe path except the internal path. Stop putting your life over there, be here now. Right now in your life, if you are not listening to yourself, you are listening to someone else. The path and the voice that you are already looking for is inside of you. So, raise your voice, even though people close to you might feel threatened that you are living your dreams. Raise your voice, put yourself out there.

Step away from people who hold you back. Follow what excites you. There is a plan in all of us. Step outside and follow the plan.

Seconds to ponder

What is your internal voice saying to you right now?

....

....

....

What is your unique story?

....

....

....

When will you step up and step out and let the world hear your voice?

....

....

....

ACTION

From today live your calling.

" When the whole world is silent, even one voice becomes powerful."

\- Malala Yousafzai

AFTERWORD

It is my sincere hope that now you have completed the 66 days of Making Changes Not Excuses, that a shift has happened in your life.

Change can be joyful and exciting, and it can be scary too. However, I have learned along the way that the only way to handle excuses is to move through them and not allow the excuses to grab hold of you.

I encourage you to maybe once per year re-read the book, as you will discover something new every time.

Never forget you are a courageous and brave spirit living on the planet during these changing times.

"You Are Full of Promise"

OTHER RESOURCES

Now that you have read Molly's Make Changes Not Excuses book you might want to explore and read her other books, audios and programmes at
http://www.harveyglobal.com/shop

To book Molly for a 'Make Changes Not Excuses' master class for teams, contact the main office on **+44 (0)151 650 8501**

To raise your game to a whole new level and create profound changes in your life and business contact Molly by email
molly@mollyharvey.com

NOTES

NOTES

NOTES

Printed in Great Britain
by Amazon

82481459R00139